Chickens Say Qué?

By J.L. Baumann

Printed in The United States of America
Link Printing, Groveland, Florida 34736
info@linkprintingcf.com

No part of this publication may be reproduced in whole or in part, or stored in a retrieval system, or transmitted in any form or by any means, electronic, mechanical, photocopying, recording, or otherwise, without written permission from the publisher. For information regarding permission, write to Post Mortem Publications, 146 East Broad Street, Groveland, FL 34736, or E-Mail: Contact@Postmortempublications.com

ISBN 978-1-941880-10-4

Translation by Kathryn Klaas

Copyright: ©Post Mortem Publications 2014
All rights reserved

~ First Edition ~

This Commemorative Edition has been brought to you by

Fetchin's Farmers Market

Produce, Pullets, Pigs & Figs

- Naturally Local Vendors -

Range Rover Chickens
Meme's Goat Cheese
Beebe's Natural Honey
Herby's Healthy Herbs

Paula's Perky Peeps
Billy's Bio Beef
Vitality Vegetables
Farmington Fisheries

~ PLUS ~

A complete line of pulchritudinous Pork products from

"The Refined Swine"

The Exclusive Producers and Purveyors of the famous

REFINED SWINE PORK RINDS

~ Also Featuring ~

White's Meat Treats, Arbuckle's Knuckles, and Peck's Pickled Pig Feet

Visit our craft pavilion and food concession area
New vendors welcome • Fun for all • Bring the whole family
Four Corners Square, Downtown New Shoatly

Contents

Digginity (Diginiddad) 2

A Tisket, A Tasket (La Canasta de Dulces) 4

Chicken Anyone? (¿Alguien Quiere Pollo?) 6

Eggsestentialism (Eggsistentialismo) 8

Chicken Picken (Decisiones, Decisiones) 10

To Nestle (Acurrucarse) 12

The Hunk of Funk (El Galán del Funk) 14

Fleedom (Libertad) 16

Souplexed (Sop-erplejo) 18

Chicken Sense (El Sentido del Pollo) 20

L'eggalese (Jerga Legal) 22

A Ringer (El Ganador) 24

Chicken Wired (Malla de Alambre) 26

An Eggsoteric Eggschange (Un Intercambio Exotérico) 28

Professing Laureates (Profesando Laureados) 30

Chick 'n Fat (El Pollito y El Gordo) 32

Hen Pecked (Mandilón) 34

Fameininity (Fama-idad) 36

Kingly Duties (Deberes Reales) 38

To Run Afowl (Meterte La Pata) 40

Eat "Firebrand" Chickens (Pollo Instigadores) 42

Deliverance (Salvación) 44

Chicken? (¿Pollo?) 46

Faux Paw (Pata Falsa) 48

Diginiddad

Este pie de pollo está divino
El granjero exclamó con gusto.
De mucho pollo está relleno
Embellecía él sin una nota de susto.

Es un trabajo preparar la masa
Dijo su esposa con placer.
La estiras con una taza
Con cuidado para no la romper.

Es el trabajo de los pollos comer
Por eso te quise decir
Que trabajes tú también
O pie no tendrás para partir.

Diginnity

This chicken pie's divine
The farmer said with relish
Plenty chicken stuffed inside
He continued to embellish

It's work to make the dough
His wife said with delight
You roll it out real slow
And pinch the edges tight

It's the chickens' work to eat
And that's the reason why
You also have to work
Or you shall have no pie

La canasta de dulces

Me levanté de madrugada
Cuando no hubo nadie por allí.
¿Dónde está mi canasta de Pascua?
No estuvo por aquí.

Alguien me la había escondido
Esto lo soñé anoche con temor.
¿Quién fue quien lo hizo?
Decían los pollitos malvados - peor.

Los huevitos pintados callados
Igual que las gomitas de fresa
Y mi canasta era tan vibrante
Rellenita de dulces espesas.

Debe haber sido el Conejo
La culpa puede ser solo de él.
Y sus travesuras no me agradan
El pollo de chocolate dijo de aquél.

A Tisket, A Tasket

So I got up bright and early
When no one was around
Where is my Easter basket?
It was nowhere to be found

I think someone has hid it
For I dreamt it in my sleep
Who was the one who did it
The malo chickens peeped

The colored eggs were silent
As were all those jelly beans
And my basket was so vibrant
Filled up with nougat creams

It must have been the Bunny
There's no one else to blame
And his antics are not funny
The chocolate chicken claimed

¿Alguien quiere pollo?

El cielo se va a caer
Proclamó el pollo sabio.
Encima de todos va a venir
El Bueno y el malo, el gordo y el flaco.

Debo advertirles
Que se preparen desde ya
Porque pronto vendrá el día
Y a nadie lo perdonará.

El pollito chiquito advirtió
Gritando caprichosamente
Que si se iba a terminar frito
Que al menos terminara deliciosamente.

Chicken Anyone?

The sky is going to fall
The chicken did proclaim
It will fall upon us all
Fat and skinny all the same

I must warn everyone
To get themselves prepared
For soon the day will come
And no one will be spared

The little chicken cried
And warned capriciously
If I'm going to end up fried
I'm going most deliciously

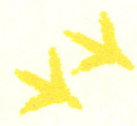

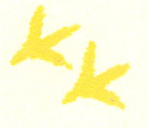

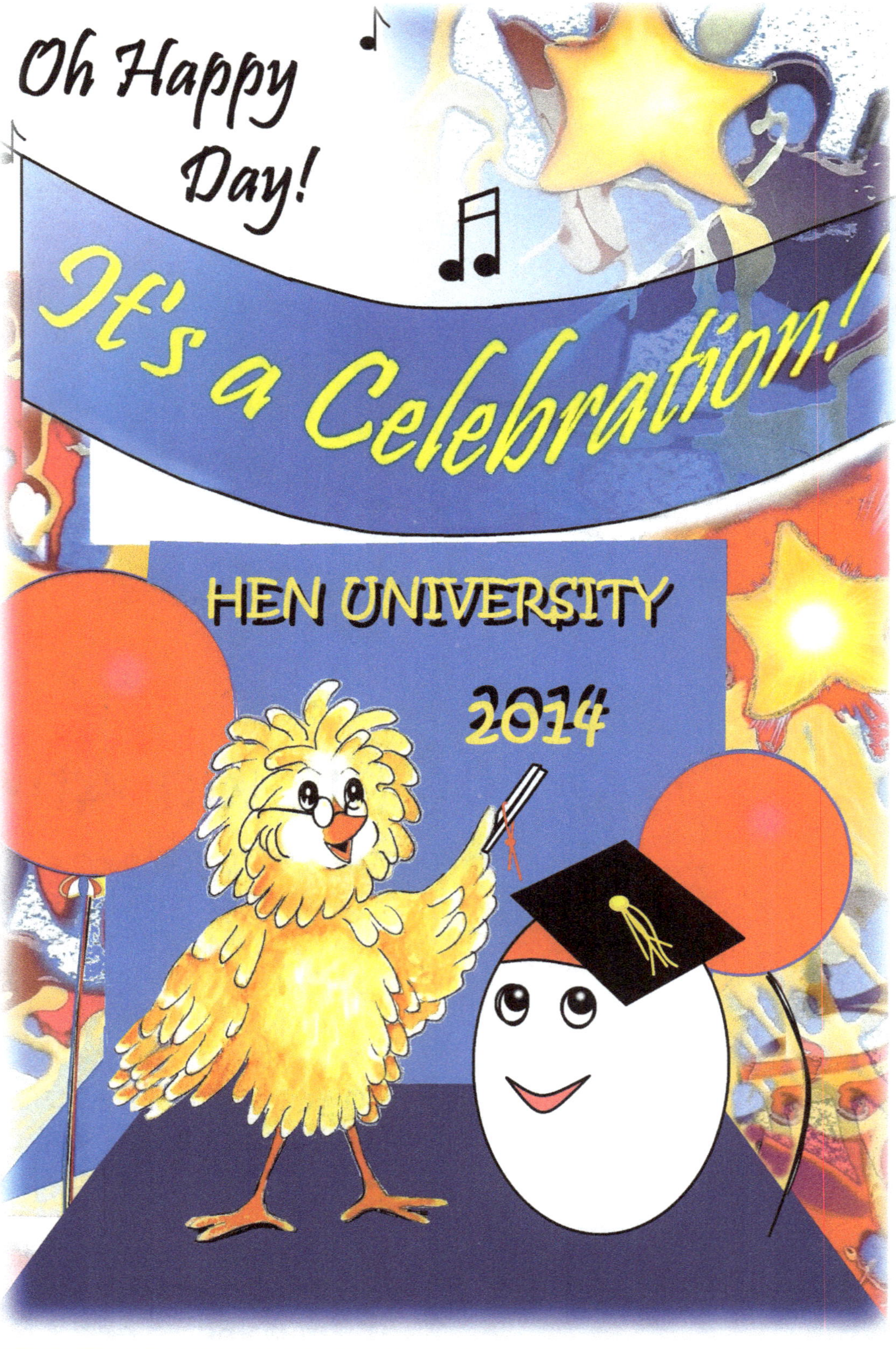
Oh Happy Day!
It's a Celebration!
HEN UNIVERSITY
2014

Eggsistentialismo

Llegué primero dijo el pollo
Pero el huevito no pudo contestar
Estuvo golpeado por silencio
Por su edad no pudo argumentar.

Al terminar la escuela de pollos
El huevito ahora negaba
Sus ideas como minúsculas
Echadas como menos profundas.

Una vez en la Universidad Gallina
Ahora, más sabio descubría
Que la vida no es adversidad definida
Sino un misterio por descubrir.

Eggsestentialism

I came first said the chicken
But the egg could not reply
With silence it was stricken
Too young to argue why

Then after chicken school
The egg now disavowed
Its thoughts as minuscule
Dismissed as unprofound

Attending Hen University
Must wiser she discovered
That life is not an adversity
It's a mystery to discover

Decisiones, decisiones

Pollo con fideos, pollo con arroz
Pollo con papas es un sabor feroz.
Pero el pollo a la barbacoa es tan suculento
Especialmente ahumado es mmm-mmm perfecto.

El pollo bien frito es siempre especial
Y justamente pensando que no hay nada mejor
Allí viene un señor con su propio plan
Pollo rostizado en un molde para flan.

Y qué de las opciones de guarniciones
Los panitos con crema son irresistibles
Los elotes con mantequilla también.
Y después de comerte uno, piensas comerte cien.

Con tantas opciones tan ricas, solo una no puedo seleccionar.
No me las puedo comer todas, pero por Dios sé que lo puedo intentar.

Chicken Picken

Chicken and noodles, chicken and rice
Chicken with dumplings, is oh so nice
But Bar-B-Qued chicken is so succulent
Especially when smoked, it is excellent

Southern fried chicken is always a treat
And as you are thinking, it can't be beat
Along comes man with a different plan
With a roasted chicken in a baking pan

And what about all the choices of sides
The biscuits and gravy you cannot deny
It's corn on the cob, salted with butter
And after you eat it, you go for another

Oh so many choices, I just can't decide
I can't eat them all, God help me I tried

Acurrucarse

Hubo un pollito chiquito
Que dio el pío pío más grato
Yo sabía que sería difícil
Y sin duda no sería barato

Tenía que ahorrar mis centavos
No quería tener que rogar
Que está relación rompía el cascarón
Y que no solo simplemente puso huevo

Al fin hice un nido lindo
De plumas suaves de plumón
Y sintiéndome realmente bendecido
Que ella había decidido quedarse.

To Nestle

There was a little chickie
Who had the cutest peep
I knew it would be tricky
And certainly not cheap

I had to save my scratch
For I didn't want to beg
This relationship to hatch
And not just lay an egg

Alas, I built a lovely nest
Feathered soft with down
And feeling truly blessed
She finally stuck around

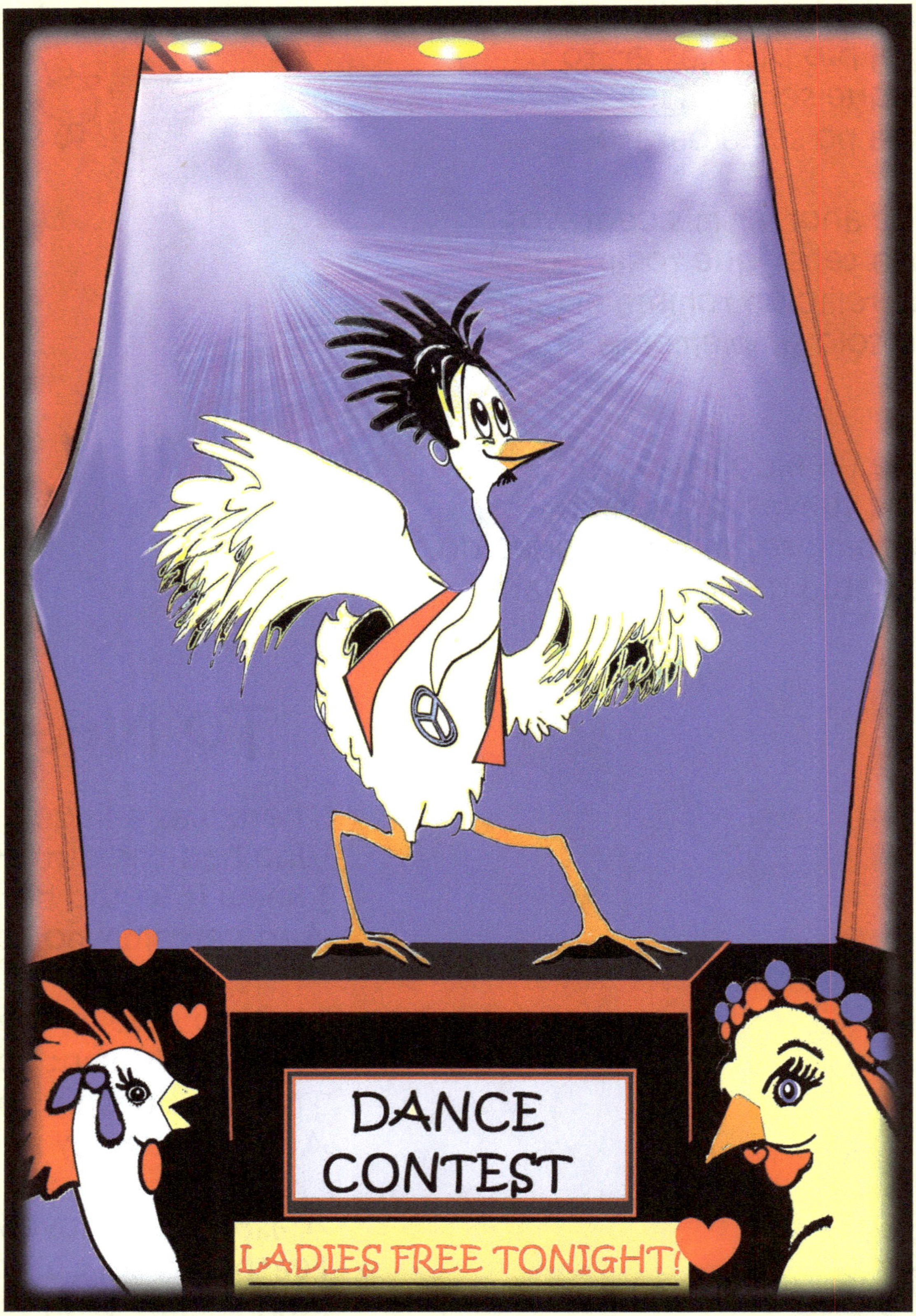
DANCE
CONTEST
LADIES FREE TONIGHT!

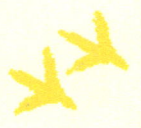

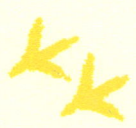

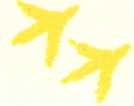

El Galán del Funk

Bailé el Pollo Loco
Por querer ser popular
Esperando que me saliera chance
Con las chicas de mi colegio

Platicaba y me pavoneaba
Como los pollitos locos hacen
Para lograr ser el bailador
Admirado por la nidada

Y así me volví impecable
Como una pieza de arte clásica
Diferente que los tontos
Que solo se metían la pata.

The Hunk of Funk

I tried the Funky Chicken
Cause I wanted to be cool
So I could have my pickin
Of all the chicks at school

I strutted and I bantered
As funky chickens do
So I could be the dancer
Admired by the brood

So I became impeccable
A classic piece of work
Unlike the other imbeciles
Who tried to do the Jerk

Libertad

Qui-quiri-quí
El gallo me decía a mí
¿Qué pude yo hacer?
Sino rendirme inequívocamente

No soy un pollo de granja
No soy parte de ninguna parvada
Soy vagabundo en mis convicciones
En tonterías dicen que andaba

El gallinero manifestaba
Que vivir en tales condiciones
Es algo tan detestable
Que preferiría me preparen en caldo.

Fleedom

Cock a doodle do
The rooster called to me
What was I to do?
Surrender unequivocally

I'm a free range chicken
Not part of any flock
I roam to my convictions
His bantering's a crock

The chicken feed implored
To live in a chicken coop
Is something so abhorred
I'd rather be chicken soup

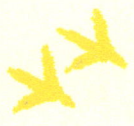

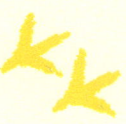

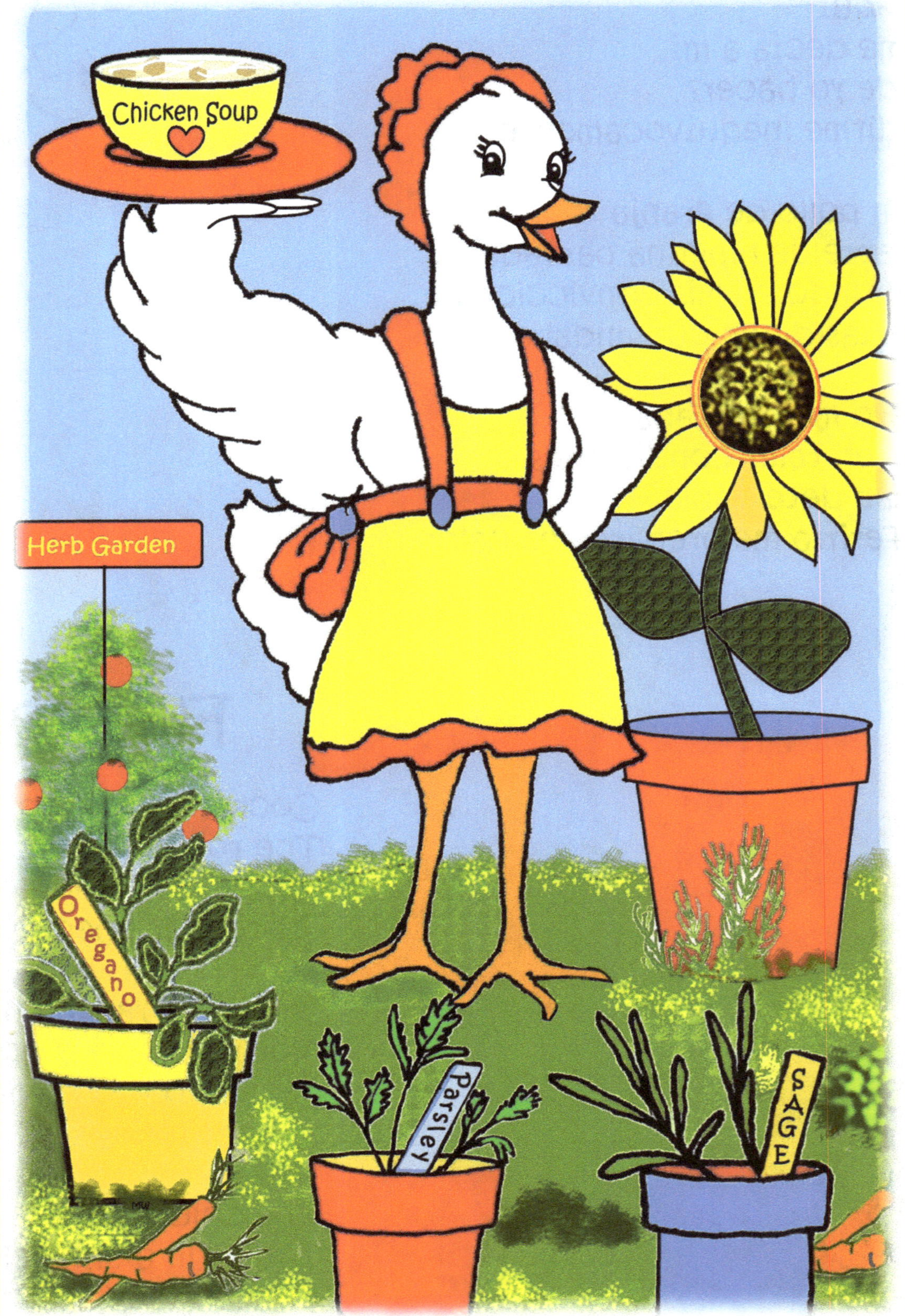
Chicken Soup
Herb Garden
Oregano
Parsley
SAGE

Sop-erplejo

Caldo de pollo necesitas
Para que te quite la gripe
Pero casi te garantizo
Que no los acompañaré

Los fideos de huevo le dan un toque
Y las zanahorias le dan sabor
Las hierbas le agregan sazón
Rico aun cuando haya calor

Es un remedio perfecto saludable
Para cuando uno esté afligido
Es una cura para la humanidad
Pero la sentencia de muerte para el pollo.

Souplexed

Chicken soup you need
To chase the cold away
And hardily I guarantee
I'll make it all the way

Egg noodles make it nice
And carrots give it flavor
As herbs will give it spice
A treat for you to savor

It's quite a healthy remedy
Whenever you are stricken
It's a cure for all humanity
But deadly to the chicken

El Sentido del Pollo

No cruces a media calle
No cruces a media noche
No cruces mientras tocas
No cruces mientras vuelas

Piensa en tu futuro
Piensa en tu pasado
Piensa en las suturas
Piensa en tu trabajo

Sabes de este pollo
Sabes de esta calle
Sabes... el tiempo pasa
Sabes del hombre muerto.

Chicken Sense

Don't cross in the middle
Don't cross in the night
Don't cross as you fiddle
Don't cross in mid flight

Think now of your future
Think now of your past
Think now of the sutures
Think now of your task

You know of the chicken
You know of the street
You know time is tickin
You know of dead meat

Jerga legal

Saludos, mi amigo plumado
¿Necesitas de mi ayuda hoy?
Soy el gran defensor de los pollos
Para unos centavos te la doy

Un pollo tiene derechos
Las leyes del pollo me las sé
Para ti, lucharé por los hechos
Por un poco de plata en la pata

El zorro había garantizado
Sobrevivir quizás podría
El bandidaje de la comadreja
Rindiéndose su propio ufanía.

L'eggalese

Hello my feathered friend
You need my help today?
It's the chickens I defend
Now let's discuss my pay

A chicken has its rights
I know the chicken laws
For you I'll dually fight
For scratch upon my paw

So the fox had guaranteed
She would perhaps survive
The nasty weasel's banditry
Surrendering her very pride

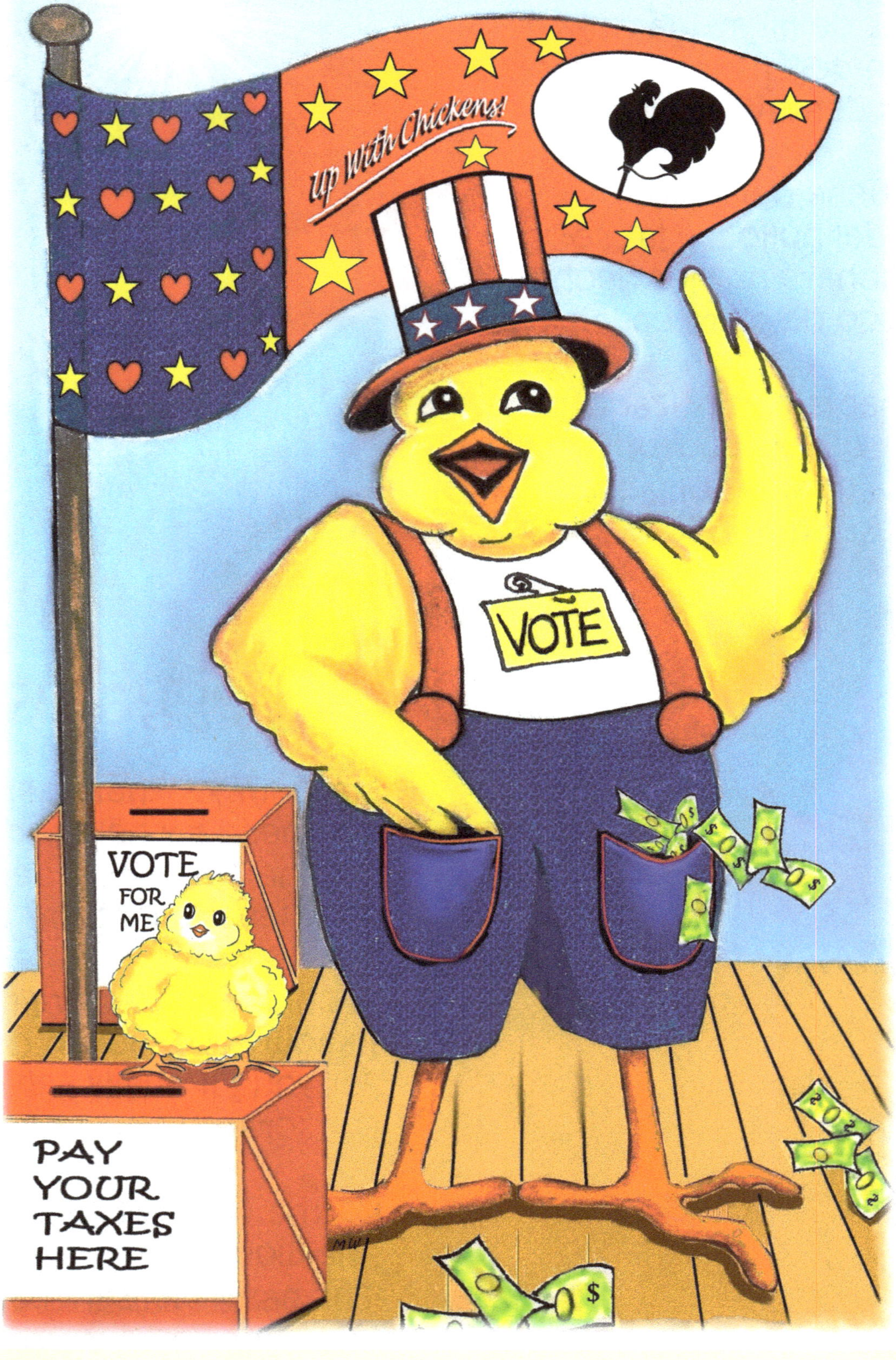
Up With Chickens!
VOTE
VOTE
FOR
ME
PAY
YOUR
TAXES
HERE

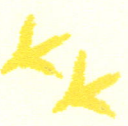

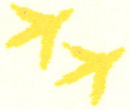

El Ganador

Levántense, pollos
El político gritó
Va pasando el tiempo
De tu voto dependió

A recaudar más impuestos
A mis amigos les pago
Y relájense ustedes
Que Se extiende mi periodo

Ollas llenas de pollos
Me comprometo así
Si se van pateando
No me afectará a mí.

A Ringer

Up with the chickens
The politician cried
Cause time is atickin
On your vote I rely

For I need more tax
To pay all my friends
And you can relax
As my term extends

Pots full of chickens
I promise they'll be
So, some go akickin
-It won't affect me

Malla de alambre

Soy una gente, el pollito informó
No, eres un pollo, la gallina aclaró
Soy libre como los pájaros, el pollito declaró
No, te tienen cercado, casi se desesperó
¿Está la gente cercada?, insistía en preguntar
Los que son pollos sí, la gallina observó.

Chicken Wired

So, I'm a people, the little chicken stated
No, you're a chicken, the old hen related
I'm free as a bird, the chick now declared
No, you're all fenced in, to know despair
Are people fenced in, asked the little bird?
All who are chicken, the old hen observed

Un intercambio exotérico

Los pollos entendieron
Que hay seguridad en masa
El Barrio del Pollo crearon
Para evitar que algo pasara

No invitaron a los pavos
Los pensaron algo tontos
Los pollos se unieron
Todos votando en su contra

Y así el Club de Pavo
Negándose a ser vencidos
Recordaba a los pollos
Que sus huevos no serán comidos

An Eggsoteric Eggschange

The chickens understood
There is safety in a flock
And created Chickenhood
To avoid a chicken crock

Turkeys weren't invited
Regarded to be dumb
The chickens all united
To vote them out as one

And so the Turkey Club
Refusing to be beaten
Reminded Chickenhood
Our eggs are never eaten

Profesando Laureados

Las águilas son imperiosas y tomadas con seriedad
Pero no son juguetonas
Habitualmente distraídas, y nunca jamás curiosas
De risa o desaliento
Tan misteriosas, a veces desdeñosas
Con grandiosas demostraciones
Siempre tan victoriosas, elegantes y gloriosas
Son prácticamente un cliché

Los pollos son industriosos y nunca belicosos
De día, de noche, ponen
Nunca tomados en serio y muchas veces chistosos
Los gallos atrevidos son
Siempre de mala fama, ignominiosos según les dicen
Desmayo nunca exhiben
Agradecidamente gregarios, otorgando Poetas Laureados
Algo de humor siempre proveen.

Professing Laureates

Eagles are imperious and taken oh so serious
But never want to play
Habitually oblivious, and never ever curious
Of laughter or dismay
So mysterious, and sometimes supercillious
With grandiose displays
Always so victorious, elegant while glorious
They're practically cliché

Chickens are industrious, and never bellicose
Day in, day out, they lay
Never taken serious and often quite hilarious
While roosters are risqué
Always quite notorious, reputedly inglorious
They never show dismay
Thankfully gregarious, giving Poet Laureates
Some humor to purvey

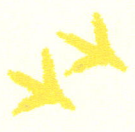

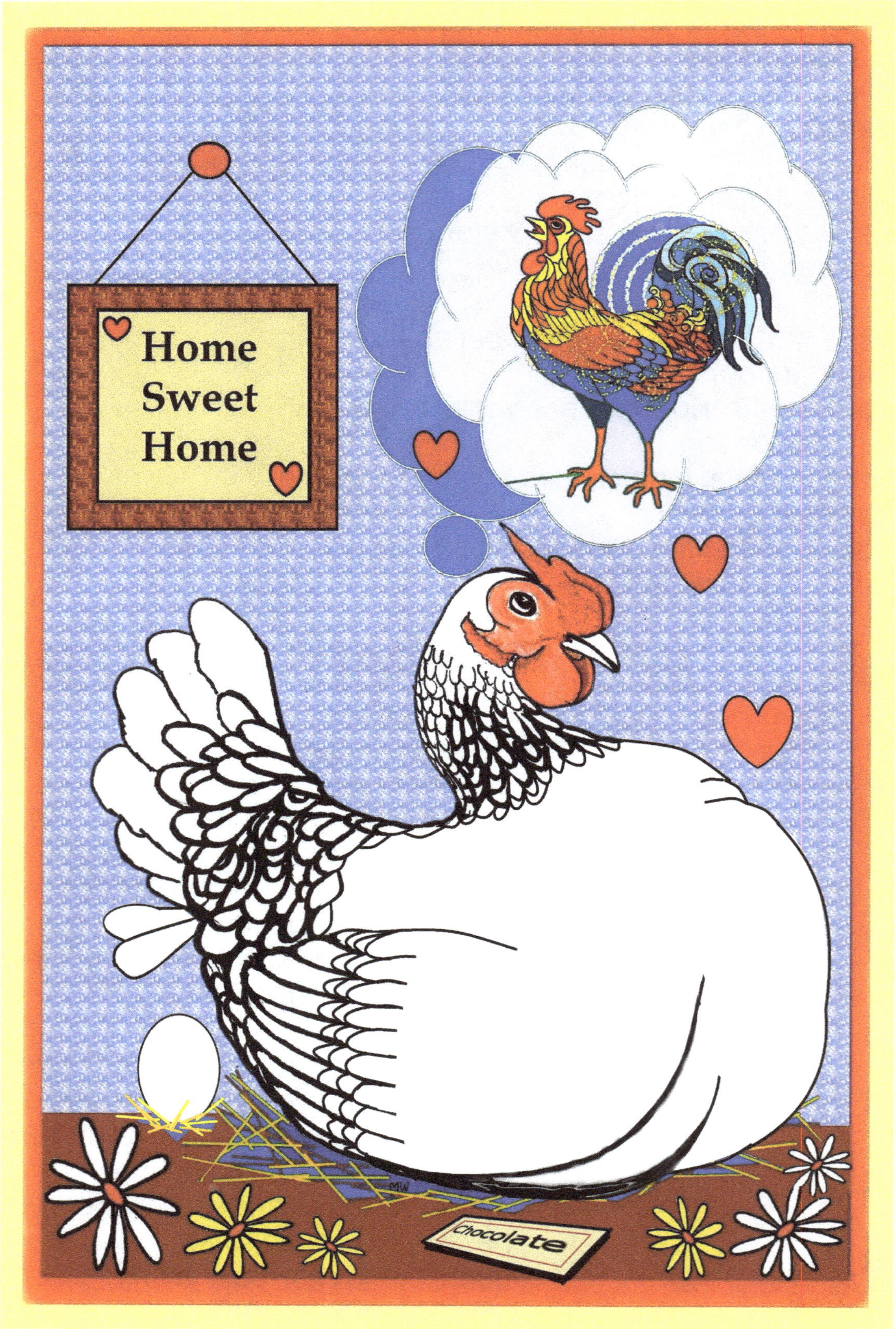
Home
Sweet
Home
Chocolate

El pollito y el gordo

Debo subir de peso
Cacareaba la gallina gordita
Que no sea muy tarde espero
Aunque me queda solo un tiempito

Hasta que el Gallo pasará
Y me entrego, estaré preparada
Para responderle su esperada llamada
Y satisfacerlo sin fin

Las gallinas son una delicia
Y tampoco soy una freidora
Quizás no soy tan nutritiva
Pero son mis gorduras que él sí adora

Chick n' Fat

I have to gain some weight
Clucked the big fat chicken
And I hope it's not too late
Tho I know that time's atickin

For the Rooster will come by
And I submit, I'll be prepared
To answer his beckon cry
And satisfy him without end

Spring chickens are delicious
And certainly, I'm not a fryer
So perhaps I'm not nutricious
But it's my fat he doth desire

Mandilón

Por todos lados cloqueaban
Picoteando buscando una lombriz
Picoteando hasta que no aguantaban
Hasta que ya les dolía la nariz

Los gusanitos se habían huido
Esperando evitar su destino
Ahora cloquean consternados
¿Qué más podrían haber esperado?

Que simplemente aguanten
Que un pollo los picotea
Preferían buscar estiércol
Y con esto emprendieron su viaje.

Hen Pecked

The chickens clucked about
Pecking for a juicy worm
Pecking until all pecked out
Until it was confirmed

The worms had run away
Not wanting to be pecked
Clucking now in great dismay
What did they all expect?

The worms to just endure
A clucking chicken pecking
They'd rather find manure
And off they went a trekking

Fama-idad

El huevo fue puesto con deleite
Con mucho cariño lo puso
Su felicidad no tuvo límite
Pero nadie más estuvo

La gallina se carcajeaba
Todos lo deben de saber
Y se reía con mucha presunción
Mi huevo los va a vencer

Ella anunciaba su triunfo
Ambiciosamente con todos presentes
Y pronto vino la comadreja
Y comió su huevo deliciosamente.

Fameininity

The egg was laid with joy
Laid in the nest with care
With happiness employed
But no one else was there

The hen did cackle loudly
The others ought to know
Again she cackled proudly
My egg's the best of show

She advertized her fame
To everyone ambitiously
And then the weasel came
And ate her egg deliciously

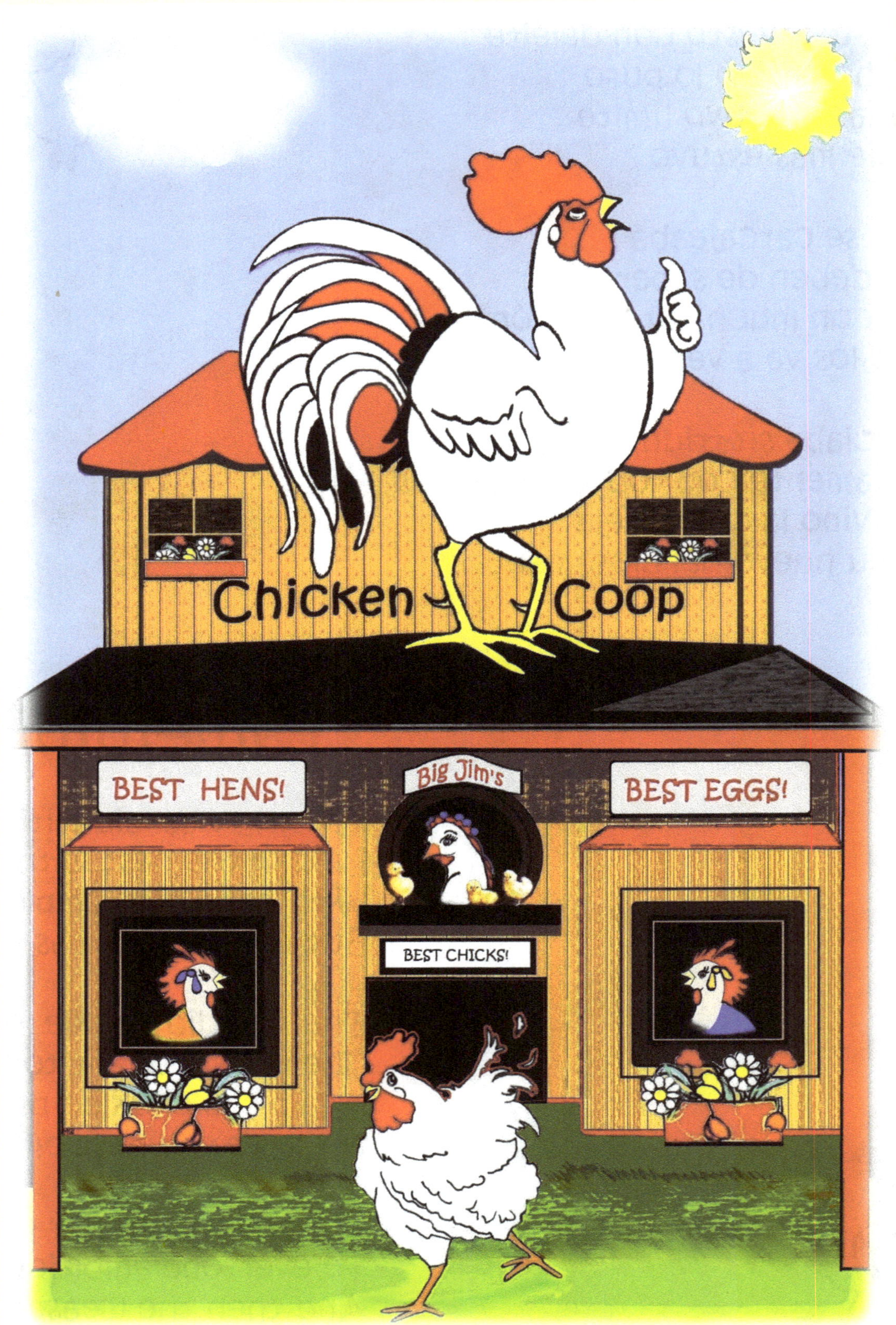

Deberes reales

No soy un pollo ingenuo
Dijo el famoso Don Gallo
Aunque el tiempo está pasando
No me deben declarar muerto

Me levanto temprano con el sol
Para atender a las bellas gallinas
Y cuando la meta se ha logrado
Lo vuelvo a hacer

Ki-kiri-kí, ki-kiri kí
Jubilarme no lo haré
Con esta tarea debo cumplir
Por ser yo su amado noble.

Kingly Duties

I'm no spring chicken
The old rooster said
Tho time is aticken
No way am I dead

I rise with the sun
To service the hens
And when I am done
I do it again

Cock-a-doodly-do
I cannot retire
This task I must do
For I am their Sire

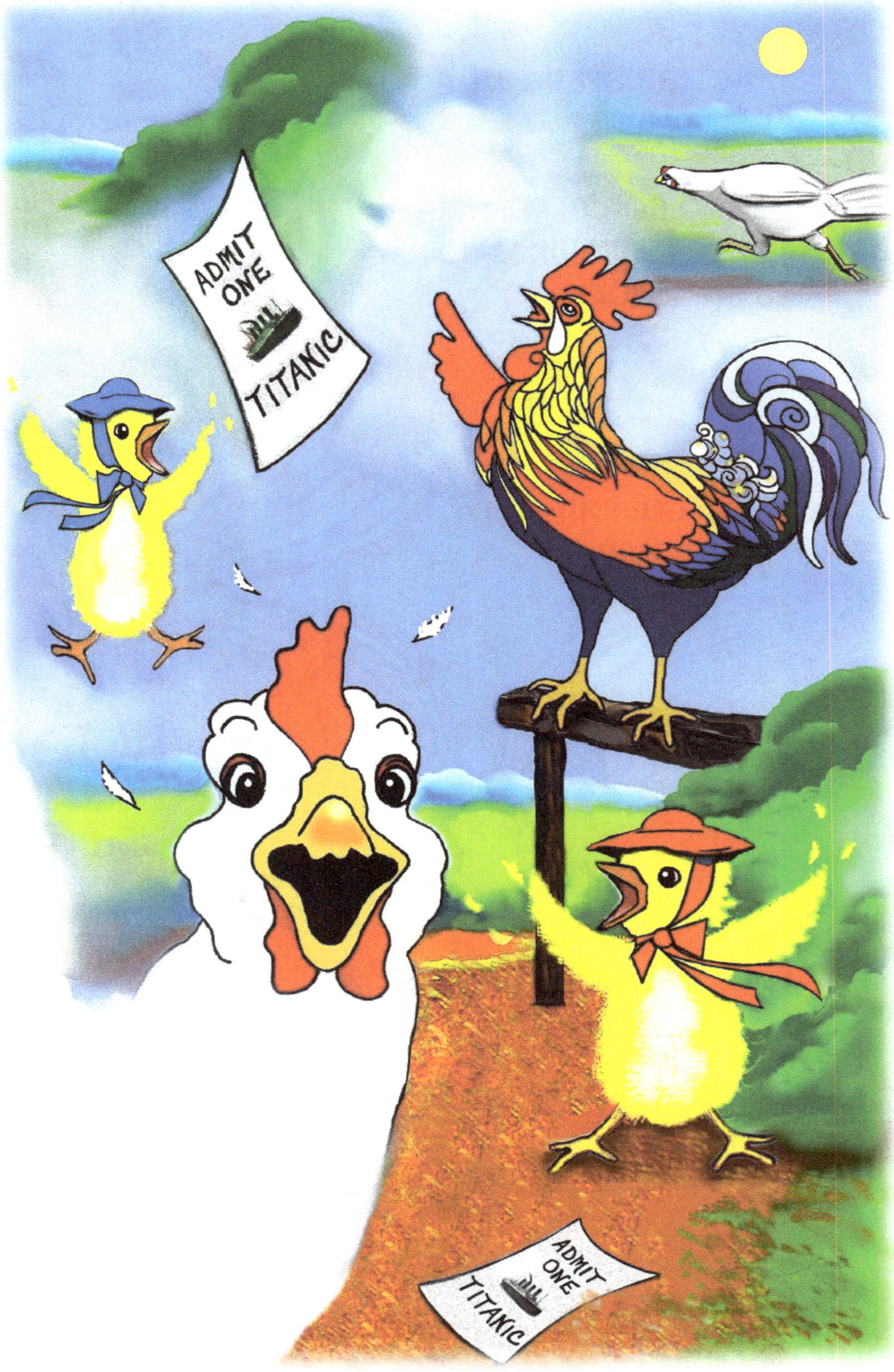
ADMIT ONE
TITANIC
ADMIT ONE
TITANIC

Meterte la pata

Los pollos daban vueltas
Sus corazoncitos en estado de pánico
Se había encontrado un boleto
Regalando un viaje en el Titánico

Posado arriba lo vi todo
Un gallo dijo con orgullo
Es el fin para ustedes
El tráiler condenaba

Pronto les llegará
Con certeza manifestó
Nada de lo que hagan
Cambiará este hecho.

To Run Afowl

The chickens ran around
Their little hearts apanic
A ticket had been found
For a ride on the Titanic

Perched high I saw it all
A rooster said with pride
It's curtains for you all
The trailer did decry

It's coming soon to you
It certainly conveyed
And nothing you can do
Can pray this fact away

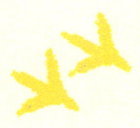

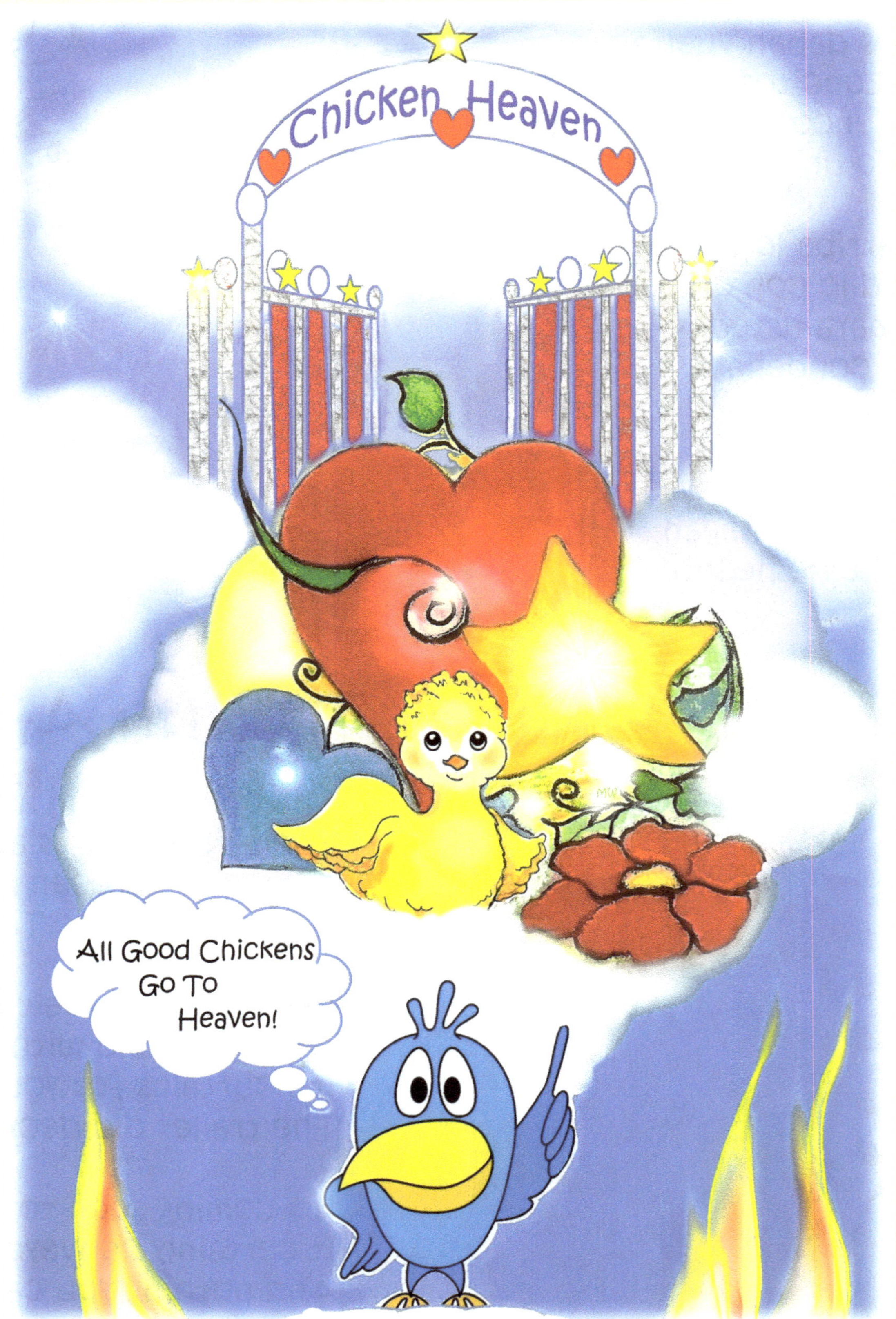
Chicken Heaven
All Good Chickens Go To Heaven!

Pollos instigadores

¿Tendrán los pollos un alma?, preguntó el pastor a su parvada
¿Y sabrán que se les acerca el fin al encontrarse en una cacerola?
¿Qué me tienen que decir, mis queridos amigos plumados?
Creo que todo depende de que si hoy confesaran sus pecados

Algunos pollos huyeron, aterrorizados con un miedo mortal
Estando yo aquí con ustedes, sabían que el fin se acercaba
Estando atiborrados de concentrado, ellos no rezaban
Hasta que al fin entendieron el significado de preparado

No tiene que ver con su cena, con zanahorias, maíz y arveja
Le toca caldo hervido cuando Dios se pone molesto
Así que la pregunta en sí es si los pollos tienen alma
¿Estás preparado para testificar que los pollos no saben?

Y ahora se preguntan a sí mismos- ¿tengo alma de pollo?
¡El Diablo está preparado! ¿Sientes las llamas lamiendo?

"Firebrand" Chickens

Do chickens have a soul, the preacher asked his flock?
And know the end is near, as they're put inside a crock?
And so my feathered friends, what do you have to say?
I guess it all depends, did you confess your sins today?

Some chickens run away, quite terrified in mortal fear!
As I submit to you today, they knew the end was near!
Gorged to death on feed, they didn't say their prayers!
Then finally they understood, the meaning of prepared!

It's not about your dinner, with carrots, corn and peas!
It's boiling broth for you, whenever God ain't pleased!
And so the question really is, do chickens have a soul?
Are you prepared to testify, that chickens do not know?

So now you ask yourself, -do I have a soul of a chicken?
The Devil is prepared! -do you feel the flames a-lickin?

Salvación

Se llamaba Cluki
Era una en un millón
Sus plumas acolchadas
Con una cola robusta

Súbase a mi percha
Carcajeaba un día
No es una iglesia
No hay necesidad de rezar

Claro que cumpliré
No me tienen que rogar
Y con esto se dobló
Y un huevo le salió.

Deliverance

Her name was Cluckie
She was one of a kind
Her feathers all fluffy
With a buxom behind

Come up to my perch
She cackled one day
Now it ain't a church
So you need not pray

Of course I'll deliver
You don't need to beg
As then she bent over
And out came an egg

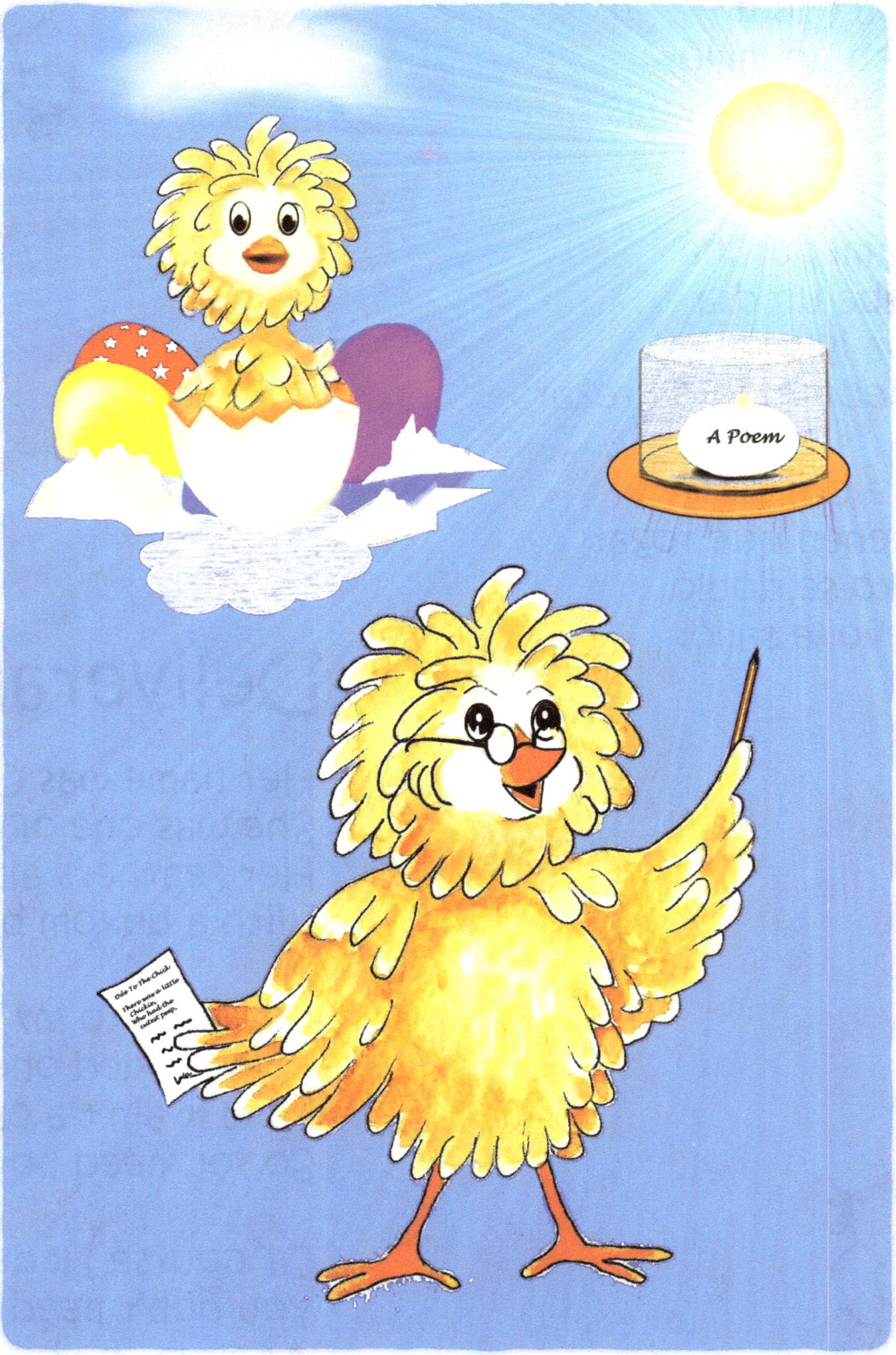
A Poem
Ode To The Chick
There was a little Chickie,
Who had the cutest peep.

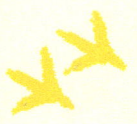

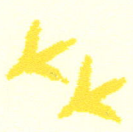

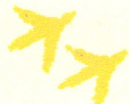

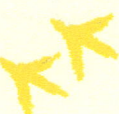

¿Pollo?

Quiero redactar un poema
Dijo el pollito.
Un poema que sea mío
Lo escucho en mi mente

Sería genial
Si lo pudiera anotar
Algo profundo
Que pienso poner a incubar

Y para siempre escrito
Mi poema será alabado
Y todo sobre un pollo
Que quería ser atrevido.

Chicken?

I want to write a poem
The little chicken said
A poem to call my own
I can hear it in my head

I feel it would be great
If I can scratch it down
Thinking I can incubate
Some poetry profound

And so forever written
My poem was extolled
And all about a chicken
Who wanted to be bold

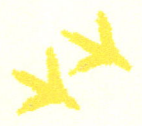

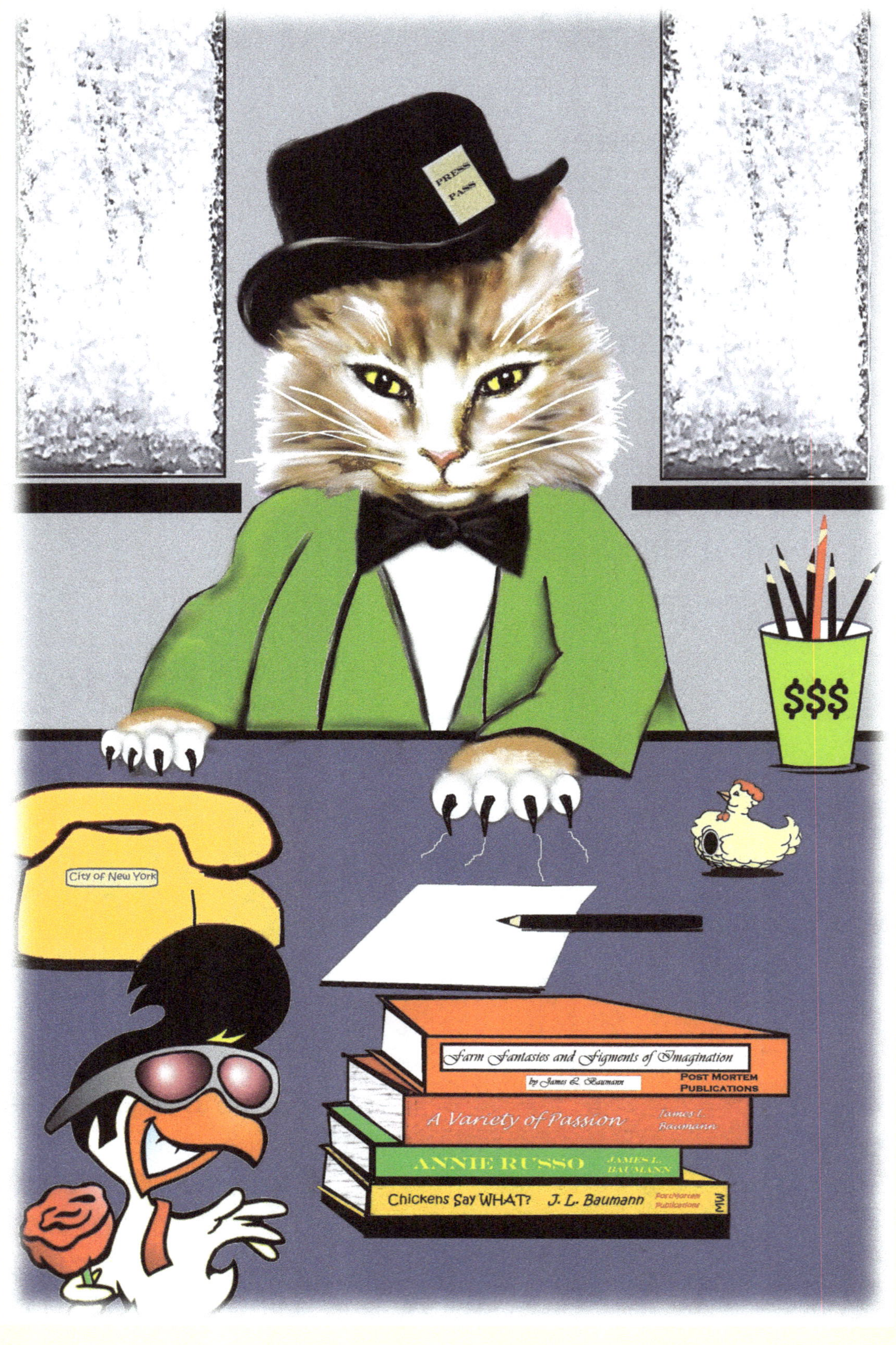
PRESS PASS
$$$
City of New York
Farm Fantasies and Figments of Imagination
by James L. Baumann
POST MORTEM PUBLICATIONS
A Variety of Passion
James L. Baumann
ANNIE RUSSO
JAMES L. BAUMANN
Chickens Say WHAT?
J. L. Baumann

Pata falsa

Un crítico de Nueva York manifestó
Que los pollos no pueden volar
Creo que fue cruzado
Con una gata callejera de por sí

Los pollos, sí pueden volar
Igual que los gatos citadinos
¿Verdad que el señor no tiene precio?
Es un crítico que da hasta pena

Los pollos lo consideran chistoso
Picando en la tierra
En búsqueda de dinero
Sin darse cuenta de su mala educación

Faux Paw

A New York critic stated
That chickens cannot fly
I think that he was mated
With an alley cat nearby

Chickens aren't flightless
Like cats think in the city
But isn't he just priceless
He's a critic to be pittied

Chickens find him funny
Just pecking in the dirt
Pecking for some money
Not knowing he's a jerk

The Full Bull Fertilizer Co.

Believable, TX

For Crops or Cows Your Choice

- Propagation Brand Products
- How Now Cow Conceptions
- Majestic Meadow Muffins
- Max's Mature Manure

We Deliver Satisfaction

~ Sign Up For ~
'It's Nature's Way' Webinars
www.bulloneybenders.con

FRED & FANNIE'S FEED SUPPLY

Certified Dealers
of
Cow's Cud Brand
Dosey Doats Oats
Beak's Chicken Scratch

THEY NEED TO EAT, SO WE CAN!

Gluten, OK

Willie's Well Drilling
~ Have Rig, Will Dig ~

Pump Repair & Replacement

"We Drill Well"

Diggers, SC

Call THurston 5 - 8686

Cackle's Eggs

Home of
"The Big End First"
Premium Eggs

Let Us Lay Some On You!

Bedsprings, AR

Mammy's Country Cookbooks

Mammy says -
Taint no better eatin' nowhere!

~ Learn how to ~

Bar-B-Que Bodaciously
Fry That Fresh Caught Fish
Cook Up Collards Quickly
&
Immortalize Your Grits

Collect The Whole Set! Now Available On-Line!
www.mammy.mom

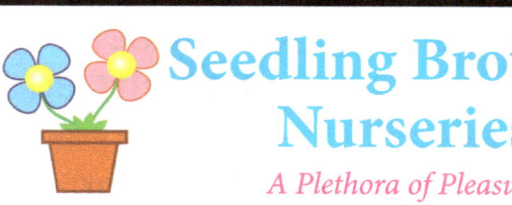

Seedling Brothers Nurseries

A Plethora of Pleasure

'Berry Delicious' Plants
Grandpa's Shoe Trees
Flora's Famous Bloomers
Rays's Radiant Bulbs

Call for Catalogue...................1-800-HAY-SEED

The Hartland
Farm Supply Company

Quality, Quantity, and Quick Service

- **Chick N' Fat Fencing**
- **Ouchless Branding Irons**
- **Kickfree's Milking Stands**

If'n we ain't got it
You cain't get it!

- **Forget Me Not Come-Alongs**
- **Barbie's "Prick-Free" Wire**
- **Woodchuck Brand Chainsaws**

A whole slew of locations - everywhere
Home Office - New York City, New York - Not!

Franchises Available

The Happy Tractor
New - Used & Aftermarket Parts

Visit Our 'You Pull Em' Graveyard
All Makes and Models

Hard to find parts from the Nomo Tractor Company of Detroit, MI

**Now Two Locations:
Box Blade, IN
and Harrow, CT**

'Since 1912 - Till Forever'